Bone OF MY Bone

AND

Flesh OF MY Flesh

BY
RICKY ALLEN

Tiffany Wilkins,
May God's Love
continue to shine
upon you! *Ricky All*
10/11/99

ISBN 0-7392-0269-3

Printed in the USA by

MORRIS PUBLISHING

3212 East Highway 30 • Kearney, NE 68847 • 1-800-650-7888

Dedication

I joyfully dedicate this book to:

- ∞ My Babies (Tiffany, Rhonda and Chancelor)

- ∞ My Best Friend (Lou)
- ∞ My Mother (Lillian) and Grandmother (Shirley)

- ∞ The Immanuel Family Worship Center of Jacksonville Arkansas

- ∞ All Readers

When all has been said and done, the only thing that remains in this life is what we've become to one another.

TABLE OF CONTENTS

ೞ FORWARD ೞ

Because of his obedience to the call of God to "plant a church" in the city of Jacksonville, Arkansas, I have been blessed to experience the leadership of Elder Ricky Allen. He is a leader chosen by God and commissioned by the Holy Ghost. He has compassion for the Lord's people and is committed to ministry. His burden for the family, the strength of his faith in God's order, and his hope for the restoration of relationships are evident in this book.

This practical guide to interdependent relationships reflects God's order for mankind. In communicating with Pastor Allen throughout the writing of this great book, it was evident that he depended solely on the direction of the Holy Ghost.

Many times he would relate how the Spirit of God stirred his inner being and began to pour out of him the next chapter of the book. It is therefore no surprise that the author uses a style that is much like the teaching of our Lord, who taught by use of parables. He uses the familiar, often experienced, situations of life to bring about understanding. He identifies issues that are common to relationships and shares a more excellent way of resolution.

This writer, who declares that the Holy Spirit is the author, shares God ordained principles that have the power to build families and destroy the yoke of divorce. Those who willingly break up the fallow ground of relationships and allow the seed of these principles to germinate will reap a fruitfulness that far surpasses average or ordinary experiences.

This is not just another book to add to your library of collections. It is the book to draw from time and time again. In it you will find hope for the future of the family, help for relationships and strength for interdependence. Read it, apply its principles and be richly blessed.

Deaconess Lou Jean Turner, BS, MA
Administrative Assistant, Immanuel Family Worship Center

ᛒᚩ PREFACE ᚷᚱ

After experiencing one of life's most tragic storms, the demise of a meaningful relationship, I stood looking at the remains of my life. I then asked the Lord, "What do I do?" "What do I tell people when my own life is in shambles? He said to me, "Show them how to keep the same thing from happening to them."

He then began to inspire the content found in this book. It is my unequivocal proclamation that the Almighty God is the Author. I am only the scribe who humbly submitted to his inspiration.

Through my weakness I have learned to humbly obey. I have asked for many things that I might enjoy life. He has given me life that I might enjoy all things. He has spoken to me in times when I didn't want to hear. He has led me in times that I did not want to follow.

There is no way I can thank Him for His constant companionship; nevertheless, I give to you the inspiration He has given to me.

I pray that *Bone Of My Bone And Flesh Of My Flesh* will inspire you to seek God's will in whatever relationship you engage in. It is practical and yet so powerful. It is common sense; nonetheless, not common practice. It is indeed a gift of hope and restoration to any interdependent relationship.

Receive the blessing of God! He is Wonderful! He is Almighty! All Praises belong to Him!

ಬ INTRODUCTION ೆ

One of the greatest problems facing society today is the disintegration of meaningful and purposeful relationships. The dilemma of our day is that we have become better at replacing our families than we have at improving and maintaining them.

We see constant assault within relationships rather than peaceful resolutions. Homes have become war grounds rather than safe havens. It appears as though we have gained a false sense of autonomy and have taken our destiny into our own hands. Truth is; we can not guarantee the end results of our lives any more than we can guarantee the rising of the sun.

Such misconception started in the Garden of Eden when deception made its grand appearance (Genesis 3:1-4). Selfish disobedience disrupted the first interdependent relationship. Humanity ignored and willfully violated God's instruction in the garden. That is when sin (through selfishness) entered and thus separated humanity from God.

Satan has no new tricks. Notice how Satan particularly approached only one person (the weaker) in the relationship. Weak in that she was vulnerable and impressionable not simply because she was female. He then began to question her understanding of God's order (Did He really say that you could not eat from any tree in the garden?). He went on to see if she would compromise those orders (You will not surely die). From there, He (The

Serpent) challenges her value for those orders (God just does not want you to be like Him). He presented something false as though it was true which led to a tragic end. After all, this is what deceit does for us. The challenge was an insult to her pride. As a result, she reacted selfishly and transgressed God's law.

Satan is using the same instruments of isolation and deceit today as he used in the beginning. He (Satan) uses such craftiness to present God's order for our lives as something confining and dictatorial. As a result, many lose their focus and compromise God's intended purpose for their lives and relationships.

God never intended it to be this way. From the beginning of time until now, He constantly proves His love to humanity. God loved us so much, that He gave His son in order to reconcile and restore us to our position and purpose in Him. We are indeed His children and His desire is that we function in interdependent relationships in a way that reflects His divine order.

Many of us desire wonderful relationships, however, do not learn how to properly function in them. Perhaps we do the best we can with what we know. More important than not knowing is the willingness to learn. Willingness is the key to discovery. The Bible says, "Now finish the work, so that your eager willingness to do it may be matched by your completion of it, according to your means. For if the willingness is there, the gift is acceptable according to what one has, not according to what he does not have (II Corinthians 8:11-12 NIV).

God takes all that we have (abilities) and develops it (capabilities) in order to reflect His will for our lives. He does not expect any more of us than He has given us. It is wonderful to know that He has given us all things that pertain to life and godliness. He has made us to be partakers of his divine nature. He has given to us great and precious promises.

We are all that God (through His word) says we are. We can do everything His word says we can do. We must not allow human frailties to discourage us from reflecting God's plan for our lives and relationships. We can not preoccupy ourselves with comparisons to others. We must be willing to apply ourselves to a more excellent way. We must possess the innocence and zeal of a child eagerly inviting and awaiting the next opportunity to learn and experience new adventures.

Bone Of My Bone And Flesh Of My Flesh is a practical guide to building wholesome inter-dependent relationships through unselfish love. It calls to remembrance God's Divine Order for such relationships.

This book is not a miracle worker unless you allow The Miracle Worker to work on you. You should not read it with the intent to change someone else. In reality, the only person you can change is you! It is not meant for those individuals who seek to find fault and to excuse themselves from the responsibility of an interdependent relationship. Nevertheless, it is for those individuals who will be brave and daring enough to look neither to themselves, nor to the influence of others but look to the eternal Word of God.

Such focus is the key to unleashing the shackles of a misdirected, mediocre and perhaps miserable relationship. Whether you have been married for years and are seeking renewal and reinforcement within your relationship, or whether you are contemplating marriage for the first time, allow *Bone Of My Bone And Flesh Of My Flesh* to direct you to God's Order for your relationship. By doing so, you can experience God's great and precious promises. You can enjoy heaven on earth!

Ricky Allen
Sherwood Arkansas

~ CHAPTER 1 ~

CHOOSING YOUR OWN ADVENTURE!

"Take your life in your own hands and what happens? A terrible thing: no one to blame..."
                                                        -Erica Jong

Choosing Your Master

*L*ife is full of choices. Each day we are faced with making decisions that will somehow affect the balance of our day. What will I wear? What will I have for breakfast? What route will I take to work? These are a few routine decisions; the fact is that decisions are necessary. Some require more attention and deliberation than does others.

Perhaps three of the most important decisions one will ever make in this life are:

- Who will be your Master?
- What is your Mission?
- Who will be your Mate?

A misdirected decision in any of these areas can lead to a misdirected and empty life.
You have the freedom of choice; however, you must know the destiny of your decision.

 Enter ye in at the strait gate: for wide *is* the gate, and broad *is* the way, that leadeth to destruction, and many there be which go in thereat: Because strait *is* the gate, and narrow *is* the way, which leadeth unto life, and few there be that find it (Matthew 7:13-14 KJV).

While this scripture is speaking of entering into the gates of eternal life, it also represents the freedom of choice on earth.

- Broad is the easy and most popular way. The fact that everyone seems to embrace it does not make it right (*verse 13*). The end could lead to destruction! Destruction of values and principles: Destruction of integrity: Ultimately the destruction of meaningful relationships.
- Narrow is the way that leads to life. In comparison to the broad way, few find the life given in the straight and narrow way. The challenge here is to not conform; rather, be transformed by renewing your mind daily.

While many of us are living, we have not entered into life.

From my childhood I grew with hopes and dreams. Those hopes and dreams included being a minister, a manager, a husband and a professional athlete (In no particular order). As I grew to adolescence I lost focus on what I wanted. Some might even say that I was too young to really know what I wanted. I guess it was that mentality that led me to trying to gain an identity among those who were going nowhere. I found myself doing things only because I wanted others to accept me.

I recall a day when I stood wondering what to do with my life. I was living but nothing seemingly made me happy. I had an inward emptiness that would not go away. The day came that I did not like what I had become. While I was yet young (sixteen years old), I knew that I was breaking principles that my parents taught me. I was misdirected and living without a purpose. Even though I was an honor student, all-star baseball player and varsity basketball player, I had a vast emptiness inside. I had chosen an adventure that led to superficial happiness and eventual destruction. My status had become my master. I did not know myself; therefore, I could not really love anyone nor could I love myself.

One day a couple of high school classmates came up to me and began to share the love Christ had for me. They began to share ways I could respond to His love; firstly, by accepting him as my savior. My first reply to their words was that the temptation was too strong. They then showed me a scripture found in I Corinthians 10:13. This scripture let me know that temptation was common and that God loved me so that he would not allow Satan to tempt me with more than I could endure. It also assured me that God would make provisions for me to escape temptation. At that point, the word of God erased my excuses for not choosing Christ as my Master.

A few days passed. My emptiness then became a craving for fulfillment. I didn't know how it was to happen. I just knew that I wanted something greater for which to live. One day some other classmates who went to the same church invited me to a revival. I made all kinds of excuses for not going. The time came and I had to make a choice. I wanted direction. I wanted purpose.

On Tuesday, January 1980, I left a basketball game at half time to attend the revival. All I knew was that I needed help. I was not in judicial trouble nor were things going bad. I needed a greater power! I was making a real mess of my life.

As the minister shared the word of God, I felt life coming to my soul and substance to the emptiness. I would like to share the power of those words with you.

 *There is* therefore now no condemnation to them which are in Christ Jesus, who walk not after the flesh, but after the Spirit. For the law of the Spirit of life in Christ Jesus hath made me free from the law of sin and death. For what the law could not do, in that it was weak through the flesh, God sending his own Son in the likeness of sinful flesh, and for sin, condemned sin in the flesh: That the righteousness of the law might be fulfilled in us, who walk not after the flesh, but after the Spirit. For they that are after the flesh do mind the things of the flesh; but they that are after the Spirit the things of the Spirit. For to be carnally minded *is* death; but to be spiritually minded *is* life and peace. Because the carnal mind *is* enmity against God: for it is not subject to the law of God, neither indeed can be. So then they that are in the flesh cannot please God. But ye are not in the flesh, but in the Spirit, if so be that the Spirit of God dwell in you. Now if any man have not the Spirit of Christ, he is none of his.

And if Christ *be* in you, the body *is* dead because of sin; but the Spirit *is* life because of righteousness. But if the Spirit of him that raised up Jesus from the dead dwell in you, he that raised up Christ from the dead shall also quicken your mortal bodies by his Spirit that dwelleth in you. Therefore, brethren, we are debtors, not to the flesh, to live after the flesh. For if ye live after the flesh, ye shall die: but if ye through the Spirit do mortify the deeds of the body, ye shall live. For as many as are led by the Spirit of God, they are the sons of God (Romans 8:1-14 KJV).

From such penetrating truth, I realized my problem:

- My Sin produced separation from God and condemnation
- My sin was ruining my interpersonal relationships
- My sinful nature did not seek to please God
- I could never be strong enough to resist the lust of the flesh, the lust of the eyes and the pride of life without God's spirit regenerating my mind and heart.

I also realized God's answers to my problem:

- Choosing a life in Christ
- Choosing freedom from spiritual death
- Choosing His direction for life
- Accepting a heritage with God

I realized that I was no longer a servant to sin; however a Son of God. I could choose my own adventure. I then accepted responsibility for my life and exercised faith in the redemptive work of Christ.

I chose a new walk (lifestyle). I chose to commit my life to the Lordship of Jesus Christ. Life took on a new meaning and literally a new direction for me. While I have had many other major decisions to make in my life, Christ's preeminence is a lamp unto my feet and a light unto my path.

You might ask what does this have to do with interdependent relationships? What does this have to with me? The answer is everything.

The most important interdependent relationship you can have is your relationship with God. I refer to this type of relationship as a "Divine Vertical Relationship." It consists of all correspondence between man and God. Sin disrupts the harmony within this relationship and leads to deceit, as well as, spiritual death.

Sin does not only disrupt your relationship with God; it also disrupts your relationship with others. I refer to this type of relationship as a "Horizontal Relationship."

When you choose to make Christ your Master (Divine Interdependent Relationship), you choose to live a harmonious adventure with God. The relationship we have with our Heavenly Father should transcend all other relationships.

Jesus Christ is the nucleus of Divine Interdependent Relationships. He advocates our relationship with The Heavenly Father, as well as with others. He provides:

- A Common Bond (Reconciliation)
- A Shared Likeness (Mediation)
- A Common Focus (Facilitation)

Remember! Sin separates and destroys relationships first by separating and destroying the individuals. It is the path of least resistance. The pleasures of Sin are deceptive and render relationships barren.

The will of God should be the inspiration for all you do. When you learn to be responsible in your relationship with God, you can be the same in all other relationships.

God had a purpose in mind for you when He created you. The only true way to know your mission is to know Him as your Master. You must not allow the term master to intimidate you. God only does that which is in the best interest of his servants.

 Here I am! I stand at the door and knock. If anyone hears my voice and opens the door, I will come in and eat with him, and he with me (Revelation 3:20 NIV).

God does not impose His will upon you. Through His word, He reveals His will to you. His only desire is that you accept it. He then guarantees that He will come in and share with you. When you permit Him to be your Master, you can move on to discovering your Mission on earth!

- He is knocking at the door of your heart
- Open up and receive Him
- Share in God's Divine Order and Purpose for your life

What an opportunity! What an adventure!

80CB

Choosing Your Mission

*C*an you remember saying to others, "When I grow up, I'm going to be a..." Ironically many have reached adulthood and still do not know what they want to be. While they live, they have not come into the purpose for which they live. If you do not know what you want to do, chances are you will do nothing. If you do not know where you want to go, any road will get you there. One road is just as good as the other. You don't know if you have come or gone. You are just wandering; hoping to end up "somewhere."

God created each of us as creatures of great intelligence and endless possibilities. He created us in *his image* (righteousness, peace and joy) and in *his likeness* (compassionate, unselfish and just). In order for you to realize those endless possibilities you must be willing to subscribe to the plan created by the great Architect of Humanity.

I beseech you therefore, brethren, by the mercies of God, that ye present your bodies a living sacrifice, holy, acceptable unto God, *which is* your reasonable service. And be not conformed to this world: but be ye transformed by the renewing of your mind, that ye may prove what *is* that good, and acceptable, and perfect, will of God (Romans 12:1-2 KJV).

The verb "present" in this verse means to commit one's body for service conclusively. A living sacrifice indicates the necessity to make such a commitment while you have mental, physical and spiritual experiences that constitute your existence. There are two examples of living sacrifices in the Bible.

- Abraham offered Isaac in obedience to God (Genesis 22). The record will show that God had a *Ram in the Bush* when he saw Abraham's willingness to obey.
- Jesus Christ gave his life as a ransom for the sins of the world in obedience to His Father's will.

You must passionately seek your purpose. It is reasonable! Do not compromise nor conform to the expectations of an ungodly society. To conform means to allow the world to control your thinking. However, to be transformed represents a change from within.

You must allow God to control your mind in order for you to satisfy a mission that is pleasing in His sight. Not only should you present your body as a vessel for His use, you should also denounce your selfish will. Say as Christ said to the Heavenly Father, *"Not what I want done, but Lord do what you want to do with me* (italics mine)." God will take your humble submission and develop character within you that is pleasing in His sight.

I am reminded of a young boy who realized his mission. He did not conform. He spent his childhood on his father's farm tending sheep; however, went on to become the greatest King in Israelite history. Yes, I am talking about David. A mixture of both good and bad filled his life. No Bible character fully illustrates the moral range of humanity, as does David. We see his success, as well as his failure. My point is; David had a mission. He was convinced that God was the littérateur of his mission. He started at a young age committing to the lessons learned during his journey to becoming the servant God had created him to become. Through much adversity and human frailty, David remained focused on his mission.

- He realized that He was just a vessel that God would accomplish His purpose through.
- He gained courage from tending his father sheep (I Samuel 17:34-45). He translated learning into living.
- He was willing to face life's challenge (I Samuel 17:37).
- He used what he had instead of armor that was not tested and proven effective for Him (I Samuel 17:39).

Just as David pursued and committed to his God given purpose, you must do the same. You too must be a *Giant Killer*. You must become all that God created you to become.

Preparation proceeds blessings! The process of becoming and discovering often requires us to move away from our comfort zones. This is a time that God will use you as a mural to distinguish his vision for your life.

An allegiance to God must be the keystone for your chosen mission. You can not truly realize His purpose for you until you take heed to His voice. Let us look at the life of Abram (Genesis 12:1-4). He heard the voice of the Lord and was willing to respond.

Abram refused to be drawn to the contention of man. Notice how he told Lot to choose his own adventure. Abram was content in taking whatever land Lot did not choose. He believed God for his purpose and made decisions based on his allegiance to God and His appointed purpose (Genesis 13).

Do not spend your time trying to become someone you are not. Spend time praying and earnestly seeking to find your God appointed mission. When you become what God, created you to become, you are an asset to any interdependent relationship. Live your life with a conviction! Live it with Faith in God's promises concerning you! Enter into life and that more abundantly!

~ CHAPTER 2 ~

CREATED TO CLEAVE...NOT COMPETE!

The process of Cleaving gives birth to "Us" without destroying "Me"-Ricky Allen

From the ground up!

*A*fter God reviewed all He had created and declared it "good," He concluded that it was not good for the male to be alone. Man needed someone with common form and function. The operative word here is *Common*.

While man had dominion over every beast of the field and every fowl of the air, there was no common form or function. God realized that man needed friendship, fellowship and intimacy from someone corresponding to himself; therefore, He made the unique creation of the woman.

Our Society can be no stronger than the relationships we build with our family and fellow citizens. Relationships are unique; however, they all must go through a dynamic process of Forming and Storming before they can perform and become fruitful. These are important steps in building healthy interdependent relationships.

Forming

The Forming phase of interdependent relationships is a time when two people come together and gain a common knowledge of one another. It is a time to discuss and compare thoughts, principles, values, goals and ideas.

Many people force relationships rather than grow into them. In order to prohibit such a social tragedy, one must be willing to start from the ground up and become friends. The forming phase must begin with a genuine friendship.

᛭ঌ

"Ah, the beauty of being at peace with, another neither having to weigh thoughts or measure words, but spilling them out just as they are, chaff and grain together, certain that a faithful hand will keep what is worth keeping, and with a breath of kindness blow the rest away."

- Arab proverb

᛭ঌ

The American Heritage Dictionary, Second College Addition defines a friend as, "A person whom one knows, likes and trust." During the Forming phase of the relationship, it is important that each individual focus on becoming the type of person that another would want to know, like and trust.

Friendship is not about demands or controlling the interest of another. It is about comradeship, companionship, and communication. Each of these words began with *Com*, which is Latin for "together." Comradeship literally means "together in the same chamber or room;" companionship literally means, "taking bread together;" communication literally means, "possessing together."[1] Togetherness must possess a love that the Greek New Testament calls *Phileo*. *Phileo* is a cherishing love that expresses willful acceptance and respect for another.

Phileo is the willful acceptance and respect of another. It is about mobilizing shared principles and values that will serve as a foundation to a more meaningful and growing relationship. While sharing is perhaps the key, togetherness certainly turns the key. It requires a commitment to a common purpose. In order for individuals to experience the life that togetherness brings to interdependent relationships, there must in many cases be a paradigm shift.

We must not try to make the Forming phase one of lifetime commitment or sexual intimacy. Often it is at this phase many find themselves trying to commit to someone they do not know, like or trust. You must not confuse feelings with reality.

Routinely people enter into relationships, impetuously becoming lovers rather than becoming friends. This type of love relates to the more primitive part of humanity...Biological parts that can be blind to relational factors.

You should seek to have a friendship that grows and matures in companionate love. Passionate love is very important; however, there are many variables that could influence one's feelings. Authentic friendship is vital to healthy interdependent relationships.

There must be a commitment to companionate love even if you do not feel that constant, intense level of energy... Energy that causes you to feel like your heart is about to come through your throat...The kind of energy that vibrates the very inner part of you.

At creation, God intended for the male and female to be together in every sense of the word. He made them to know, like and trust one another.

The process of knowing, liking and trusting involves:

- **Actively listening without criticizing**
  A priceless jewel to any relationship is the ability to communicate. Actively listening is an important part of effective communication. It is a deliberate action of interactive sending and receiving information. Actively listening and being physically present when someone is talking to you is not synonymous. While you might not always enjoy what another person says, you must give that person the joy of talking to you and not at you. You can expedite a person's willingness to trust you when you show that you are in tune to what they are saying. Active listening says:

ℕℓℜ

Come! Talk to me,
Share with me the content of your heart.
I am interested and trustworthy,
Within me, your best interest will never depart.[2]

ℕℓℜ

In order to become an active listener, one must practice effective listening skills. Here are a few helpful hints to actively listening.

- Assume a friendly posture. This indicates that you are open to conversation. Try to eliminate any thing that might create space or tension between you.

- Make constant eye contact with the person you are talking to. By this, you show the other person that you are a part of the conversation.
- Seek clarification on things said that might be unclear to you (Example: What do you mean by...)
- Show visible consent (nod of the head, smile) that you understand what the speaker is saying to you.
- Paraphrase what you hear without taking away the meaning of what the speaker said (Example: Let me see if I understand what you are saying...)
- Ask open-ended questions (what, how, when) in order to facilitate open communication.

  It is important that you do not judge or criticize what the speaker is saying. You can disagree with what the other person says without judgment or criticism. Criticism prohibits open communication.

- Accepting without demanding

  You should seek to know the person for who he or she is and not for whom you want them to be. When we demand that people become a certain way, it sends a message to the other person that says, "I am not good enough." Avoid comparing the object of your friendship to others. The power to change and recreate another individual resides with the Almighty God, Father and Creator.

- Giving without expecting

  Be a giver. If you give only because you want to receive, you miss the whole purpose of giving.

A gift opens the way for the giver and ushers him into the presence of the great (Proverbs 18:16 NIV).

One of the most valuable lessons I have learned in life is the lesson of giving without expecting. I have always been a person who enjoyed giving. However, it was not until experiencing much frustration and often feeling unappreciated that I realized that I was giving for the wrong reasons. I also realized that I was giving because I wanted the other person to appreciate me. I was not giving because I wanted to show my appreciation for the other person. Now that I understand the purpose of giving, I also experience great exhilaration in giving. When I need something to make my day or to reaffirm my self worth, I give and expect nothing in return. I am a gift; therefore, I freely give.

• Laughter without intimidation

The Bible says, "A merry heart doeth good *like* a medicine: but a broken spirit drieth the bones (Proverb 17:22 KJV)." The ability to laugh is an essential part of any healthy interdependent relationship. Do not take yourself so seriously that you forget how to laugh. If it is not a matter of life and death, it is not that serious. Laughter is medicinal. Look for the bright side of every situation.

If you do not find any humor in a situation, create it! Things could always be worse. The lack of humor dehydrates relationships. The relationship then becomes frail. It becomes more work than fun.

The Forming phase of the relationship should be about relaxation and establishing an affinity or an association with one another. Laughter facilitates such an environment. Fill your relationship with it.

When God had completed his creation of the female, He brought her to the male Adam. He then presented her to man as a valuable gift.

Let us examine Adam's appreciation of the female. Adam first made an identity with her in Genesis 2:23. Adam is saying, *this is a part of me. She is what I am made of. She substantiates my existence. I like her.* He placed value upon the woman by saying, *that because she came from me, I will name her Woman* (Italics Mine). God made woman suitable or comparable as a partner in life. As the man and woman began to experience the Forming phase of their interdependent relationship they expressed shared meaning and value. They came into a greater sense of life and purpose now that they had formed. They became friends! They went about in the garden and were not ashamed. This indicates an acceptance of each other just as they were.

I must point out that at this point in their relationship, there is no record of physical intimacy.

When relationships begin with a mere attraction and progress to a physically intimate level without going through a natural process of growth, they often lead to endless frustration, pain and regret.

Example:
You are feeling somewhat erogenous and pursue physical intimacy; however, you have nothing in

common. It is like building a house without pouring the proper load bearing footing.

I would like to suggest the following questions as a litmus test to the foundation of your friendship.

- Do you spend quality non-sexual time together?
- Do you have fun together?
- Do you share activities and interest?
- Do you know and like each other?
- Can you freely talk to each other?
- Can you confide in one another?
- Can you depend on one another for help?
- Can you depend on one another's loyalty?

If you can truly answer yes to these questions, you are well on your way to the next phase of the relationship. This phase is the Storming phase. It is a phase of revelation and advanced knowledge of the other person.

৪০০৪

Storming

No two independent forces can truly come together without experiencing this phase. It is like two independently large bodies of water coming together to form an even larger body. Each body of water has a unique composition. Each possesses great power; however, the process of tranquillity can be rough.

The Storming phase of the relationship is one in which couples are trying to balance expectations with behavior. Masculine and feminine personalities compound the challenge of harmonizing.

When you do not give adequate time to the Forming phase of the relationship, Storming can prove to be very vexing. It is a time when many little idiosyncrasies surface. Perhaps these things were not evident during the Forming phase and you say to yourself, "I did not see this side of him or her earlier." There is no need to panic at this time. It could be that there is a misalignment of expectations and behavior.

Often expectations are unclear and ambiguous. As a result, behavior seems inappropriate. When it comes to aligning behavior with expectations, you can do the "Right Thing" or the "Wrong Thing." When it comes to executing, the same applies. You can do things "Right" or you can do things "Wrong." Simply putting it, you can do the "Right Thing the Right Way." You can do the "Right Thing the Wrong Way." You can also do the "Wrong

Thing the Right Way," as well as, the "Wrong Thing the Wrong Way."

The Expectation/Behavior model (Fig.2-1) is a tool that can help evaluate and bring to light the misalignment of expectation and behavior.

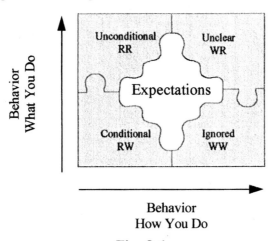

Fig. 2-1

 A Right Thing the Right Way is when it is more important for you to be what another needs than it is for you to satisfy yourself.

When individuals align behavior with expectations, they establish a foundation for mutual requirements. Such requirements are uncompromising and unconditional and do not seek reciprocity. Both parties should esteem them highly and should allow these mutual requirements to govern their behavior. Throughout the Forming and Storming phase of interdependent relationships, you should constantly seek to understand and be understood.

You must then be willing to behave in ways that are fruitful for your relationship.

 A "Right Thing" the "Wrong Way" is when you know what the other person expects; however, your behavior is conditional. It manifests itself in the following manner: I will be what you expect if you do this or that for me. This behavior is deceptive. Perhaps you are doing the right things but for the wrong reasons.

 A "Wrong Thing" the "Right Way" is when expectations are unclear. You find yourself doing what you think the other person wants without really discussing what is important to that person. This is a dilemma in which many find themselves. They rely on past experience and influences without clarifying the present expectations. Consequently, they behave in ways that are good without becoming what the other person needs for now. It seems like nothing you do is "good enough." You must at this point clarify expectations. Do not make assumptions! Take time to ask questions.

 A "Wrong Thing" the "Wrong Way" is when one chooses to ignore the expectation of another and behaves in a way that is selfish and self centered. Selfishness is the root cause of most problems. It refuses to consider the wants and needs of others and demands that everyone meet its needs.

The Social and Cultural trends of our day have made competition a norm. We are in a time that both males and females are operating outside of traditional and stereotypical roles. While we in many ways welcome such liberation, we have not learned how to use it in concert with God's Divine Order. Gender has become a real issue in the Twentieth Century. Sadly, to say the Twenty-first Century does not look any brighter.

Gender is exploited daily. "The gender issue is not primarily a political issue--though it certainly has tremendous political impact. Nor is it a social issue--though it affects society at its very foundation. Neither is it primarily an economic issue--though it has great economic ramifications. It isn't even primarily a sexual issue--though sexuality is a central element...Gender is an issue of theology. And theology is the most foundational of all the sciences."[3]

In a quest for "equality," many males and females have lost their identity.

So God created man in his *own* image, in the image of God created he him; male and female created he them (Genesis 1:27 KJV).

Gender is at the heart of creation. It is central to the glory of God. While at creation God established hierarchy with the male and female, he intended for them to function in the best interest of the other. God created male and female equally with purpose. However, he did not create them with the same purpose. The fact is that man and woman have never been the same and never will be.

Satan constantly tries to distort the meaning of God's order for male and female and how they should function as a unit.

In a society where men are confused about their masculinity and women are confused about their femininity, there is only disintegration, disorientation, destruction and death. Ultimately the society collapses...Such confusion began most noticeably in the sixties; gathered momentum in the seventies; achieved "politically correct" status in the eighties and is at the heart of an unbelievable legal turmoil and in-your-face social engineering of the nineties.[4]

God created male and female to cleave; not compete! Competition produces winners and losers. Individuals seeking to share a life together must be careful not to fall into this trap.

There seems to be much difficulty making the transition from the social arena (Community, Work Place) and the sacred arena (Family, Home). Even though society promotes competition, individuals seeking to function as one, must realize that they are not in competition to become better than the other is; Neither are they in competition to always be right. They are not in competition to become superior by making the other feel inferior.

It is important that you know God's order for interdependent relationships. Let's go back to the beginning of creation and review a great discovery made by man.

 For this reason a man will leave his father and mother and be united to his wife, and they will become one flesh (Genesis 2:24 NIV).

To cleave is a two-fold process that establishes common form and function. It involves:
1. Splitting or breaking away.
2. Clinging, binding or making one's way.

Once man and woman understands and accepts their purpose, they can see a cause or reason to break away from former influences and relationships in order to cling, bind and establish directions for themselves.

Let's face it! Most of us have become products of our environments. We consist of learned behaviors; some traditional and some non-traditional; some right and some wrong.

When it comes to interdependent relationships, we use as an example the relationships of others: Whether it is the relationships of parents, friends or someone in the community in which we admire. I am not saying that it's wrong to use the apparent success of others as a role model; However, I am saying that it is more important to know what your relationship requires of you.

Many times we resist what God wants for us because we want others to think more of us than they ought. You must not let what you hear and see in others obstruct God's Divine Order for you and your relationship.

 And whatsoever ye do, do *it* heartily, as to the Lord, and not unto men; Knowing that of the Lord ye shall receive the reward of the inheritance: for ye serve the Lord Christ. But he that doeth wrong shall receive for the wrong which he hath done: and there is no respect of persons (Colossians 3:23-25 KJV).

There is no impressing God. God rewards obedience.

In order for you to come into your own unique and divine purpose, you must break away from former influence and advice that is not conducive to your binding and making your own way with another. You should seek to become that which is pleasing in the sight of God and not man. You should ask yourself: Is God pleased with who I am and what I present to Him?

In the book of Genesis, the male Adam established a new identity. The two became one in mind and spirit.

When you cleave emotionally and spiritually to another, you will begin acting in the best interest of that person. It does not happen instantaneously. It requires constant focus on the requirements for the relationship and a willingness to satisfy those requirements.

If you must compete in your relationship, make sure it is to be the best partner you can be. When each individual focus on being the best partner to the other, they supply the relationship with a constant source of energy, and endearment. If you spend more time looking for the ideal partner than you do becoming the ideal partner, the chance of the relationship being ideal is marginal.

Now that we have laid a solid foundation from the ground up, let us move on and begin the framework to a more intrinsic level of growth and development.

~ CHAPTER 3 ~

WHERE IS THE
B-O-N-E?

"Oh, the miraculous energy that flows between two people
who care enough to get beyond surface and games."

-Alex Noble

Blessings

*7*his section of the book strongly emphasizes fruitfulness within interdependent relationships. This phase is one that authenticates belonging.

What we provide in life is essentially a work of art. There are plenty of artists. We should observe those artists who articulate the splendor of life itself. They use their tools to express the inexpressible. Without a brush or palette, they depict life with bright colors. Without a knife, they sculpt the splendor of existence. Without a scale, they create music for us all. Without choreography, they engage in the dance of life.

At birth, God gives each of us tools in order to author a life of beauty. We can use these same tools to perpetuate ugliness and ruin. We should hope to take life's canvas and reflect the beauty of blessings. Do no harm; however, help if you can. Tangible works of art fade with time. The passing trends may discredit them; however, intangible lives of love and *blessings* last forever! The New Testament word "Blessing" comes from two Greek words: eu, meaning "well" and logos, meaning "word."

It is important to realize the power of the tongue. The tongue can bring life or death to your relationship. Its words are resounding whether they are good or bad.

Bless those who persecute you; bless and do not curse (Romans 12:14 NIV).

Blessing is not something you try. Neither is it something manipulated by others. It's something you become! Perhaps, the Four "B's To Blessings" (Fig. 3-1) can help you get started.

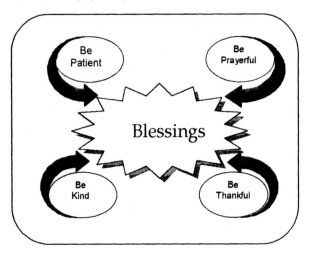

Fig. 3-1

We manifest blessings through *words* and *behavior*.

1. Be Patient
Patience is an effective force of power. You gain patience through experience. Patience allows another to be different while at the same time accepts the fact that it too is different. In order for you to experience a true since of belonging with another,

you must learn to understand and share in those differences. The Bible puts it like this, "Be completely humble and gentle; be patient, bearing with one another in love (Ephesians 4:2 NIV)." Patience is the ability to endure for long periods of time without complaining.

This does not mean that you do not get annoyed. It means that you are willing to endure differences with an understanding.

I guess I can better explain the concept of patience through the male female shopping experience. You are talking about true annoyance!

The real problem is that men and women view shopping differently. Men have the "Hunt and Kill" mentality. They are the providers for the family. When the family needed meat, the man went out into the woods; found an animal; shot and killed it. That quick, the shopping was over!

A woman on the other hand is pampering. She made home warm and inviting. She has to feel a certain emotion about shopping. A red dress is not a red dress by the time you arrive at the shopping center. You might find yourself going all over town to find a red dress. I never realized that there were so many variations of red until I tried shopping with a woman! Usually we both ended up annoyed. I seemingly rushed her in and out of stores. She seemingly wanted to look all over town for a red dress when the first one she saw looked well to me.

The real issue was that we both needed to understand each other's definition for shopping and develop a tolerance when we shared in that event.

If you find yourself constantly complaining, you have not become patient. The Bible personifies patience and the effects of such powerful force. Let us consider: "But let patience have *her* perfect work, that ye may be perfect and entire, wanting nothing (James 1:4 KJV)." We must let patience have *her* complete work in us in order for us to become complete. If you do not develop endurance for differences, every little thing becomes a big problem.

2. Be Prayerful

"A prayer in its simplest definition is merely a wish turned heavenward." - Phillips Brooks

There are enough external challenges to your relationship. You should not add to them by constantly complaining about your significant other's shortcomings. Constantly complaining causes you to only see the flaws of the other person. You must realize that your significant other needs your blessings through prayer.

 The end of all things is near. Therefore be clear minded and self-controlled so that you can pray. Above all, love each other deeply, because love covers over a multitude of sins. Offer hospitality to one another without grumbling (1 Peter 4:7-10 NIV).

It is dangerous to allow irrational thinking and anger to consume you. The adversary is not your partner. The adversary is Satan! He comes to steal the joy, kill the influence and destroy the harmony of

God's divine purpose for your relationship. You only make it easier for him when you respond in ways that are unproductive. If no one is praying, wherein is the salvation of the relationships? We must be willing to talk to God, as well as, allow God to talk us regarding our significant other. Complaining does not effect a genuine change; while prayer most definitely does.

Do not pray with the intent of changing the other person; however, pray with a willingness to place the outcome in the hands of God. God can do much more than we could ask or think if we will truly seek to please him in all our ways. By doing so we gain patience to accept those things we can not change; Valiancy to change the things we can and Insight to know the difference.[1] So, do not make grumbling about your significant other a habit. Have a talk with God! The more you consult Him the more he will direct you into a love that covers the many faults of the one you love. When you are effectual and fervid in your prayers, you can create an inseparable bond.

3. Be Kind

"Guard within yourself that treasure kindness. Know how to give it without hesitation. Know how to loose it without regret; how to acquire without meanness. Know how to replace in your heart by the happiness of those you love the happiness that may be wanting to yourself." - George Sand

To become kind is to become naturally attracted to the best interest of another. You should not do so as an attempt to manipulate or control another's behavior. Your motive for kindness must result from the authentic joy you receive in showing favor toward your significant other.

The Bible says, "A kind man benefits himself, but a cruel man brings trouble on himself (Proverbs 11:17 NIV). When you become kind you can manage the spirit of another. By this I mean you know how to respond to the disposition of another, as well as, create an environment that can extinguish the most hostile situations.

Never use anger as an excuse to become unkind in thought, words or deeds. How does one benefit from anger? If the mind conceives it, then the mouth speaks it. Eventually, the body achieves it.

 Do not repay evil with evil or insult with insult, but with blessing, because to this you were called so that you may inherit a blessing. For, "Whoever would love life and see good days must keep his tongue from evil and his lips from deceitful speech. He must turn from evil and do good; he must seek peace and pursue it (I Peter 3:9-11 NIV).

To hurt the one you love is to inadvertently hurt yourself. If you want to experience true joy in life, you must bless others by being considerate and sympathetic. When you bless your significant other with patience, prayer and kindness, it is no effort being thankful.

4. Be Thankful

Thankfulness is the process by which you seek to eliminate the negative and accentuate the positive. In it we learn to be content in all things. Contentment in no way suggests mediocrity; however, contentment is learning to value and learn from whatever predicament you find yourself. By being thankful, you express appreciation for the positive attributes of the other person. You must be ever mindful that things could be worse. Thankfulness is the demonstration of acceptance.

 In every thing give thanks: for this is the will of God in Christ Jesus concerning you (I Thessalonians 5:18 KJV).

Regardless to how your significant other is, they are yours. You made the decisions to share your life with them. Consider them as a gift. Cherish them! Bless them without reservation! Be Patient; Be Kind; Be Prayerful and Be Thankful.

Oneness

"Just as the wave cannot exist for itself, but must always participate in the swells of the ocean, so we can never experience life by ourselves, but must always share the experience of our life that takes place all around us."
- Albert Schweitzer

Independence breeds selfishness. It is hard to function independently in an interdependent relationship. Interdependence fosters oneness. It requires a paradigm shift from viewing things in the single tense to the plural tense. You must not see interdependence as a compromise to your individualism; however, a compliment.

There are many philosophies that distort and discourage God's intent for us to unselfishly share our lives. Allow me to share a few of them with you.

- Greece said, "Be wise, know yourself!"
- Rome said, "Be strong, discipline yourself!"
- Religion says, " Be good, conform yourself!"
- Epicureanism says, "Be sensuous, enjoy yourself!"
- Education says, "Be resourceful, expand yourself!"
- Psychology says, "Be confident, assert yourself!"
- Materialism says, "Be satisfied, please yourself!"
- Pride says, "Be superior, promote yourself!"
- Humanism says, "Be capable, believe in yourself!"
- Philanthropy says, "Be generous, release yourself!"[2]

Yourself! Yourself! Yourself! Many are so preoccupied with "self" that they can do nothing meaningful with themselves.
Jesus says, in Matthew 16:24 *"Be wise* (Italics mine), deny yourself!"

Oneness requires an attitude that would rather give than receive. It requires humility. Humility is not the willful annihilation of self-esteem; nevertheless, it is the willful showing of differential respect toward another. The Apostle Paul said it best when he said:

Do nothing out of selfish ambition or vain conceit, but in humility consider others better than yourselves. Each of you should look not only to your own interests, but also to the interests of others (Philippians 2:3-4 KJV).

I recall talking to a young woman who had recently gotten engaged. While being engaged, provided her much joy, it also provided much apprehension. She told me that the thing she feared most was, 'loosing her identity.' She was focusing on all of her accomplishments. She had a successful career. Her fiancée had a successful career. She did not realize that they were in competition. They struggled over who made the most money and who had the finer things, etc. I explained to her that she should not view it as a lost of identity. She should see it as a compliment to her identity. I went on to tell her that if she wanted to succeed, it would take loosing a self-centered identity and discovering a greater identity in which gives birth to a life of shared purpose and meaning. This is essential to the growth and development of your interdependent relationship.

When you become one with someone in meaning and purpose, you realize a synergy (Synonymous Energy) that provides bountiful potential for resurgence and development within your relationship. Your resources, talents and abilities combined with another's resources, talents and abilities will lead to unrestricted reward.

Listen to what the Word of God has to say about oneness:

 Two *are* better than one; because they have a good reward for their labour. For if they fall, the one will lift up his fellow: but woe to him *that is* alone when he falleth; for *he hath* not another to help him up. Again, if two lie together, then they have heat: but how can one be warm *alone*? And if one prevail against him, two shall withstand him; and a threefold cord is not quickly broken (Ecclesiastes 4:9-12 KJV).

Notice how the writer of this passage of scripture mentions a "threefold cord":
- Your commitment to another
- Another's commitment to you
- God's commitment to the both of you

Herein is the essence of interdependency! Two functioning as one is much better than two being together; however, functioning independently.

More relationships are damaged from within than they are from some external force. It does not take much opposition to break harmony when the enemy is inside the garrison.

A successful relationship requires both parties denying themselves. Together they form an invincible foe. Allow God's presence to create a bond within your relationship that is not easily broken.

God designed life with companionship in mind. He retrospectively looked at creation and declared that, "It was not good for man to be alone (Genesis 2:18 NIV)." There is a connection to everything. A leaf does not fall nor a child suffers without each of us somehow being affected. There is no longer a place to hide from each other. No wall is high or strong enough to separate us from our loneliness and despair. Love is the most effective connection to all things. It possesses the power to enlighten, heal, unite, enrich and restore.[3] All we need to do is share it.

Nurturing

Interdependent relationships require effort. They are much like fine silver. Quite beautiful and valuable; however, neglect can tarnish them. Just as silver requires constant polishing and buffing in order to maintain its luster, so do interdependent relationships. While stainless steel (mediocre relationships) will do, in no way do they compare to the real thing.

One can not expect a relationship to become valuable if he or she does not invest the time necessary in order to maintain it. Relationships never die a natural death. They die from neglect and abandonment. They die from blindness and indifference and from being taken for granted. The things omitted are often more deadly than errors committed. In the end, relationships die from weariness, from not being nurtured.

We do not really fall out of love any more than we fall into it. When love dies, there is a failure to replenish and renew it. Like any other living and growing thing, a loving and wholesome relationship requires a commitment to keeping it healthy. A state of "complacently good" is as much a threat to loving relationships as is "consistently bad."

To nurture is to help grow and develop. It is the twining of blessings and edification. It is the perpetuation of kindness. We should not see our significant others as someone separate; however, a part of us.

 So ought men to love their wives as their own bodies. He that loveth his wife loveth himself. For no man ever yet hated his own flesh; but nourisheth and cherisheth it, even as the Lord the church (Ephesians 5:28-29 KJV).

We have such regard for our bodies that when experiencing affliction even as small as a scratch, we give immediate attention to the need. Do not make the mistake and hit your finger with a hammer! Every thing stops until you have pampered the affliction.

Such love for one's self should transcend into a nourishing love for another. Jesus Christ, our Lord, availed himself to the needs of humanity. He often asked, *"What do you want me to do for you* (italics mine)."

Nurturing is the constant deposit into the 'Emotional Bank Account' of the other person. If we make more withdrawals than we do deposits, eventually we will discover an empty account. You might ask, how do I make deposits into someone's emotional bank account. Well, you can start by:

- Showing concern for their concerns
- Being liberal and genuine with compliments
- Being thoughtful without an apparent reason
- Creating memories
- Loving without demanding
- Not breaching your significant other's confidence by revealing conversations meant only for the two of you

If there is a rule to nurturing, it is to study and know the object of your love and be willing to minister to their emotional needs. The word minister means to 'serve.' The greatest lesson in nurturing and servanthood is that of our Lord's. In Matthew 20:28 KJV, He emphatically stated that, "*He came not to be ministered unto but to minister* (italics mine)." He literally meant that He came not to be served; however, he came to serve the needs of humanity. He constantly deposited into the emotional bank account of others. In essence, He came to edify and not to condemn.

Edifying

"To build may have to be the slow and laborious task of years. To destroy can be the thoughtless act of a single day." — *Winston Churchill*

A house divided against its self will not stand. There is little that is more shattering and demeaning than the casual "put downs." We have become so accustomed to dealing with them that we often fail to realize how devastating they can be in the long run.

It is always bewildering in that the people closest to you often cause you the most pain. It seems as though they can be more kind, patient and understanding with others than they are with you. Why is it like that? Could it be that individuals become so common with one another that they overlook the value each brings into the relationship? Let's look at how the Bible addresses such a state.

 Let us therefore make every effort to do what leads to peace and to mutual edification (Romans 14:19 NIV).

It is essential to know the person with whom you choose to share an interdependent relationship. You know what they like and dislike. You know the things they regard as most valuable. You know the things that affect the mood swings. Wow, what knowledge! While for you to acquire such knowledge is great, it can also be disastrous when misused. You must balance knowledge with love. Love *Edifies*, it does not degrade.

The Bible tells us to "Let love be without dissimulation. Abhor that which is evil; cleave to that which is good. Be kindly affectioned one to another with brotherly love; in honour preferring one another (Romans 12:9-10 KJV)."

As you grow into an inner knowledge of your beloved, you must not exploit it through selfish and manipulative behavior. Let your love be without difference. Apply yourself to doing and saying things that will be good for your relationship. You must show a sincere desire to hear, understand and meet the needs of the other person, first and foremost.

Edification enables growth. It is essential in maintaining a harmonious interdependent relationship. Edification requires sensitivity, as well as, maturity.

Seldom do two people grow at the same pace; nevertheless, they should commit to helping one another throughout the growth process. You should attentively use your mental and physical energies to facilitate peace and mutual building of another.

Edification requires effort and constant attentiveness to affirm the positive when confronted with conflict or displeasure. The benefits of such attentiveness exceeds the temporary discomfort of laying one's pride aside in order to build another.
You should avoid using generalizations that do not apply to the object of your love.

It is true that all men have something in common as do all women; nevertheless, they are not all the same. As companions, you must see yourself as builders not demolitionists.

Imagine being the general contractor of your "dream house." Would you be mindful of the quality of material used in the building process? Would you tear walls down as fast as you erect them? Would you be more complimentary of another's home than you would your own? Remember! That dream house is a reflection of you. The end result somehow compensates for the mental and physical energies you applied during the building process.

You can find one of the most admirable displays of edification in the Songs of Solomon. It is one of the greatest love stories ever written. Scholars regard this authentication as spiritual allegory that represents the love God had for His chosen people; the love Christ has for His church; as well as, the love man and woman should have for one another.

Please listen! Allow the mutual words of King Solomon and his beloved animate your heart and soul.

❤ *Her sweet and tender words for her beloved* ❤

I am a rose of Sharon, a lily of the valleys. Like a lily among thorns is my darling among the maidens. Like an apple tree among the trees of the forest is my lover among the young men. I delight to sit in his shade, and his fruit is sweet to my taste. He has taken me to the banquet hall, and his banner over me is love. Strengthen me with raisins, refresh me with apples, for I am faint with love (Songs of Solomon 2:1-5 NIV).

❤ *His sweet and tender words for his lover* ❤

How beautiful you are, my darling! Oh, how beautiful! Your eyes behind your veil are doves. Your hair is like a flock of goats descending from Mount Gilead. Your teeth are like a flock of sheep just shorn, coming up from the washing. Each has its twin; not one of them is alone. Your lips are like a scarlet ribbon; your mouth is lovely. Your temples behind your veil are like the halves of a pomegranate. Your neck is like the tower of David, built with elegance; on it hang a thousand shields, all of them shields of warriors. Your two breasts are like two fawns, like twin fawns of a gazelle that browse among the lilies. Until the day breaks and the shadows flee, I will go to the mountain of myrrh and to the hill of incense. All beautiful you are, my darling; there is no flaw in you (Songs Of Solomon 4:1-7 NIV).

It is clear that Solomon and his bride accepted responsibility for building one another. Edification is essential to a life long and meaningful interdependent relationship. You can start by:

- Appreciating even the 'small' things in the other person
- Complimenting their efforts even if there is not apparent success
- Speaking well of them before others
- Never allowing anyone to disrespect them in your presence
- Showing respect for the other person's opinion
- Never being to proud to admit when you are wrong

Remember! One thoughtless word or deed can destroy growth that took much effort to accomplish.

When two people mutually bless and nurture one another the results are edifying. They create a union that will withstand the storms of life.

By now I hope you understand why I asked the question, "Where is the B-O-N-E?" If you are experiencing drought in your relationship and are wondering what happened, please ask yourself that important question.

Your relationship does not have to be mediocre; neither does it have to be unproductive. Restore or create a sense of belonging to your relationship and enjoy being "Bone of One's Bone"and "Flesh of One's Flesh." *Bless! Unify (Oneness)! Nurture! Edify!*

Now the relationship is truly performing as designed. Intimacy takes on a new meaning. We have laid the foundation. We have completed the framework. It is time to attach walls that will endure the elements of time and provide a serene refuge.

We often think that marriage creates the ultimate sense of belonging. Not So! Truth is, to belong as God ordained creates the ultimate marriage.

~ CHAPTER 4 ~

MARRIAGE...THE FACT AND THE FIGMENT

"One day filled with ceremonial bliss does not constitute marriage. It is only the beginning..."

*F*ormer President George Bush stated while delivering a commencement speech May 1992 at the University of Notre Dame that, "Whatever form our most pressing problems may take, ultimately all are related to the disintegration of the family. If America is to resolve our social problems, we must first resolve our families."

I must agree by saying, so goes the family, so goes the world. Strong families build strong societies. Strong marriages build strong families. Jesus Christ, the Author and Finisher of Our Faith, is the core of strong marriages.

 But at the beginning of creation God made them male and female. For this reason a man will leave his father and mother and be united to his wife, and the two will become one flesh. So they are no longer two, but one. Therefore what God has joined together, let man not separate (Mark 10:6-9 NIV).

Marriage is the ultimate manifestation of interdependent relationships. It is the *process* of two components uniting in order to function as one. It is no longer "My" money but "Ours." It is not "My" career but "Ours." It is not "My" house but "Ours." It is Not "My" children but "Our" children. Notice I said *process*. A process is a series of actions, changes and functions to bring about an end result. It is continuous progression. Processes generally consist of four fundamental components (Inputs, Knowledge & Skills, Equipment & Tools, Outputs).

It is one thing to sit and wish for the ideal marriage; however, in order to actualize it you must be a 'Prime Mover.' You must be the person to set into motion the necessities for a successful marriage. To do so can lead to outputs of heavenly results right here on earth.

The diagram below (Fig. 4-1) will point out these necessities.

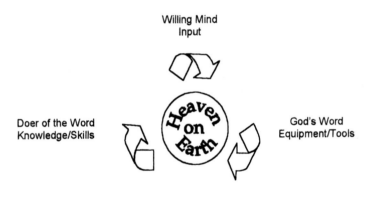

Willing Mind
Input

Doer of the Word
Knowledge/Skills

God's Word
Equipment/Tools

Fig. 4-1

One day filled with ceremonial bliss does not constitute marriage. It is only the beginning. The marriage process requires time, effort and endless learning.

It is important to acknowledge the mutation of our marital society. The man is not always that courageous leader who will put the needs of his family before his own. The wife is not always the pleasantly content homemaker who raises the children and insures that the house is a home.

The reality of marriage somewhat reminds me of the old computer jargon, "Garbage in, Garbage out." This simply implies that you get out what you put into it. While the computer has endless capabilities, it can not realize them if the user does not use his or her resources to tap into the computer's resources. Marriage is no different. It doesn't "Just Happen!"

In many marriages today, both the male and female work outside the home. The shared stress of homemaking and child raising is constantly redefining the roles of the male and female. While society has placed great emphasis on diversity, it has failed to teach two people how to properly function as one in a diverse society. Society might very well redefine the method for "Playing the Game"; however, it does not have the jurisdiction to change the rules.

God has an order for marriage. Those who embrace and obey this order must send a message that no man, system or trend will put asunder that which God has joined together.

Successful marriages have become the exception rather than the rule. A successful marriage requires a mind willing to seek knowledge from the Word of God, as well as, diligently apply the principles therein.

Clearly, millions of men and women have no difficulty "falling in love;" however, at least half find it difficult to stay in love.

The fact of the matter is that divorce is the fastest growing marital status. The number of divorced people has more than quadrupled, from 4.3 million in 1970 to 18.3 million in 1996.[1] Of those that survive legally, a large number survive in name only. This startling statistic suggests that love, let alone, is not enough to keep marriages together. After the novelty of marriage has worn off, some couples find that the roaring flame of their original desire for each other has dwindled to a mere smolder. Is it because of boredom, inexperience or fear? Do some couples simply marry for the wrong reasons?

This is not an attempt to answer the many reasons because they are as varied as are the people. Whatever the reasons, couples can revive their relationships.

A blending marriage requires the constant destruction of myths. We must attack and destroy them as quickly as television (Hollywood) and other influences produce them. Instead of spending your time dreaming and longing, you can embrace principles that will help realize the joy a willing marital relationship can bring.

It is important to understand God's Order for marriage. The relationship's well being depends upon this Divine Order. It is this order that every marital relationship should explore and build upon. Marriage is more that just an amiable thing to do; marriage possesses a higher dignity and power. It is the first event God inaugurated into his plan for society. In this Divine plan, God intends to perpetuate the human race until the end of time.

Marriage is a triune institution in which God intends to mirror the relationship shared between Him and His son (Divine Order), as well as, that of His son and the church (Earthly Fulfillment). Both the New Testament and the Old Testament, compares God's relationship with His people to that of a bride and groom (Isaiah 61:11, Jeremiah 2:12, Revelation 21:2,9).

It is important that individuals realize their responsibility to God's Divine Order and fulfill that order here on earth.

 Submitting yourselves one to another in the fear of God. Wives, submit yourselves unto your own husbands, as unto the Lord. For the husband is the head of the wife, even as Christ is the head of the church: and he is the saviour of the body. Therefore as the church is subject unto Christ, so *let* the wives *be* to their own husbands in every thing (Ephesians 5:21-24 KJV).

When you realize your position (Fig.4-2) in God's order, you can move on to know, understand and fulfill your responsibility within His order.

೮೧೮೩

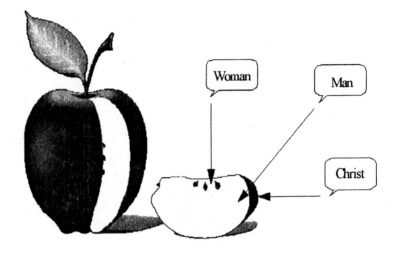

Fig.4-2

◆ The Peel-- Symbolizes Christ. He is the Head of the Church. He provides guidance, protection and security for the marriage. He always does what is in the best interest of His beloved church. He fulfills His responsibility for the church in humble obedience to God, the Heavenly Father. With Jesus Christ as the head of the marriage, we have divine providence. A marriage without Christ is incomplete and is subject to rapid deterioration as is the apple without a peel.

◆ The Flesh—Symbolizes Man. He protects the woman by representing Christ's love for his church. Christ loved the church with a love that was everlasting. He was reaching the church with a love that was:

Bone Of My Bone And Flesh Of My Flesh

- Constant because He always reaffirmed His love
- Comforting because He worked all things for their good.
- Self-giving because He gave himself for their benefit
- Unconditional because nothing can stop Him from loving
- Understanding because He looks beyond their faults and served their needs
- Unwarranted because they could never be good enough or do all the right things to become deserving of his love

♦ The Core--Symbolizes the woman. She is the reproducer and supports man's existence.
When we section an apple, we refer to it as "A piece of Apple." This is an acknowledgment that the apple is no longer complete. The same applies with marriage. A marital relationship is no longer complete when man and woman function independent of one another, as well as, God's Divine Order.

Marriage is not about convenience. To even mention the word 'submit' (Ephesians 6:22) would insult many ideals of political correctness. Clearly, God's order for your marriage is not about political correctness. It is about spiritual correctness.

You might be thinking, "Who me, Submit to Him!" I am liberated! "Who me, Submit to Her... I am the head!" Yes You!

You must realize that God's Divine Order should be the preeminent authority for all that you do. The husband and wife should submit to one another in commitment, communion and communication.

Commitment

In order to experience a marital relationship the way God intended, man and woman must yield or surrender oneself to the will or authority of another. Through marriage, the male and female entrust the most personal and most intimate part of themselves to each other. Before a man and woman can truly commit to one another, they must first accept full obligation to the purpose for which God created them.

Commitment essentially reminds me of a story I once read about two New York men who had never been out of the city. They decided that they had had it with city living, so they bought a ranch down in Texas in order to live off the land like their ancestors.

The first thing they decided they needed was a mule. So they went to a neighboring rancher and asked him if he had a mule to sell. The rancher answered, "No, I'm afraid not." They were disappointed, but as they visited with the rancher for a few moments one of them saw some honeydew melons stacked against the barn and asked, "What are those?" The rancher seeing that they were hopeless city slickers, decided to have some fun. "Oh," he answered, "those are mule eggs." The city slickers were overjoyed at this, so they bought one of the melons and headed down the bumpy country road toward their own ranch. Suddenly they hit an especially treacherous bump and the honeydew melon bounced off the back of the pickup truck, hit the road and burst open. After seeing through his rear-view mirror what had happened, the driver turned his truck around and drove back to see if he could retrieve his mule egg. Meanwhile, a huge Texas jackrabbit went hopping by and saw this honeydew melon splattered in the road. He hopped over to it. The jackrabbit then calmly stood in the middle of the mess and he began to eat.

Now here came the two city slickers. They spied their mule egg burst open and this long-eared creature in the middle of it. One of the men shouted, "Our mule egg has hatched! Let's get our mule." But seeing those two men coming toward it, the jackrabbit took off hopping in every direction with the two city fellows in hot pursuit. The two men from New York gave everything they had to catch him, but finally they could go no farther. Both men fell wearily onto the ground gasping for air while the jackrabbit hopped off into the distance. Raising up on his elbow, one of the men said to the other, "Well, I guess we lost our mule." The other man nodded grimly. "Yes, but you know," he said, "I'm not sure I wanted to plow that fast anyway."

Are you like these New Yorkians? Do you want a change? Do you want results; however, are not willing to put forth the effort to actualize the results wanted? Are you so vulnerable that you will listen to anyone regarding your relationship? Let us now look with greater inquisition at our responsibilities to God's order for marital relationships.

♫ *A Message to the Man*

Man is the being whom God intended to reflect his image and likeness. He should govern himself to God's order. The flesh of the apple is not the apple; however, it creates substance for which the peel accentuates. It covers the core and protects the seeds therein. Have you ever witnessed a head functioning independent of the rest of the body? God made you the head of woman not to dictate, manipulate or violate her. However, He has placed within your care a being and a body that substantiates your existence. You should seek to humbly fulfill your responsibility to your wife and family. You represent Jesus Christ on earth. To represent is to "stand in for" or "bring back again." God has given you a precious gift (woman). You must Bring God's Order back to your marriage by providing, protecting, and teaching in love.

Providing

If anyone does not provide for his relatives, and especially for his immediate family, he has denied the faith and is worse than an unbeliever (I Timothy 5:8 NIV).

The First Epistle of Paul to Timothy records responsibilities of various interpersonal relationships within the fifth chapter. The eighth verse reveals the necessity of providing for one's family. To become remiss in providing for your family is to denounce any loyalty to your family.

Providing for your family is more than bringing home the paycheck and giving your family all the things that they want. Your family is in need of much more than that. More importantly, you must provide for your family spiritually and emotionally. You must provide your family with a vision. You must put before them a visual image that indicates direction. Put before them a portrait of principles, values and traditions. You must provide them with qualities and features that will distinguish them from another. You must paint the picture vividly! You must paint the picture explicitly! You must provide them with a legacy!

You must assure the family that you will manage their resources prudently. You must provide them with good judgment. You must provide the cherishing love Christ has for the church.

Protecting

 Be on your guard; stand firm in the faith; be men of courage; be strong. Do everything in love (I Corinthians 16:13-14 NIV).

You hold the highest office in civilization. No! Not the Presidency of The United States of America; Perhaps not the Chief Executive Officer of some conglomerate corporate office; Not the Pastor or Deacon of a church but the head of your family. As the head of your family, you are the watchman.

The Bible says that, "The thief cometh not, but for to steal, and to kill, and to destroy" (John 10:10a). You must guard against the mendacity of Satan. He deceitfully seeks to "kill your influence, steal your joy and destroy your harmony."

Manhood is not about how loud you can roar out demands. Teddy Roosevelt once said, "A man's usefulness depends upon him living up to his ideals insofar as he can. It is hard to fail but it is worse never to have tried to succeed. All daring and courage, all iron endurance of misfortune, make for a finer, nobler type of manhood. Only those are fit to live who do not fear to die, and none are fit to die who have shrunk from the joy of life and the duty of life."

Manhood in its truest sense has very little to do with biology; however, everything with responsibility. Many homes suffer from the erosion of manhood. Many wives have become the pillars to the home because the husbands did not stand firm and provide courageous leadership. You must not passively sit and allow your family to wander down broad and barren pathways of conformity. However, you must courageously lead your family to green pastures of promise. You are the head and watchman of your family. Courageously declare as

Joshua, a mighty warrior in Old Testament history declared in Joshua 24:14c: *I will lead my house to serving the lord* (Italics mine.)"

Teaching
The home is the greatest institute of learning. All other institutes should reinforce the values and principles taught in your home. You should not expect your family to simply do what you say. Action speaks much louder than words! You must teach values and principles through precept and example.

 But refuse profane and old wives' fables, and exercise thyself *rather* unto godliness (I Timothy 4:7 KJV).

The Apostle Paul wrote these words to a young man that had the grand responsibility of establishing a church during a time of gross misdirection resulting from false teaching. The people were reverting to past unproductive and unfruitful behaviors. They exercised unsound theories and philosophies more so than they did the truth found in the Word of God. It was incumbent upon young Timothy to teach and be an example through word, conversation, charity, spirit, faith and purity.

As the head of your family you must be willing to dismiss ungodly myths and pursue godliness. Do not let anything distort the value God has placed upon the family. You are a teacher; whether good or bad, someone is learning from the example you set. Teach your family in word, conversation, charity, spirit, faith and purity.

Your home is your civilization. You must exemplify a persistent and unfailing love as you encounter the stress of family living.

As the head, you must give yourself to providing, protecting and teaching your family. Allow the love Christ has for His Bride (The Church) become your example. Do it courageously! Do it with your whole heart! Do it now!

Leave your family a legacy!

A Message to the Woman

Woman is like the seed of an apple. She substantiates life and fruitfulness. In Genesis the second chapter God referred to the woman as a 'helper.' Her purpose is divine. God made her for the man. This does not mean that she is inferior to man. The word 'helper' more accurately means 'strength' or 'power.' Such strength and power are a compliment to man. Often God himself is designated by the term strength or helper (Psalms 33:20).

God created the first woman from man's rib. This authenticates interdependence. God made woman for the man; therefore, she depended on him. Some biblical scholars observe that the earliest language of Mesopotamia and Sumerian has a word for rib that means life.[2] Man depends upon you to give birth to a life filled with substance and meaning.

You are the life of man. The Bible says, "A virtuous woman is a crown to her husband: but she that maketh ashamed is rottenness in his bones (Proverbs 12:4 KJV)." You have the ability to affect all that he does and all that he has. When you represent all God intended, you could create an environment filled with peace and comfort. As the life and glory of man, you are a priceless treasure. Give your spouse the gift of virtuosity.

The Songs Of Solomon said in Proverbs 31:18 that the virtuous woman "perceives that her merchandise is good. Her candle does not go out by night".

You must know without reservation God's intended purpose for you. You must not allow the darkness of our day to put out your light of goodness and moral excellence. Uphold a 'candle' with the luminous radiance of Trustworthiness, Industriousness and Diligence. Allow this key to God's word to direct you.

 The heart of her husband doth safely trust in her, so that he shall have no need of spoil. She will do him good and not evil all the days of her life. She seeketh wool, and flax, and worketh willingly with her hands (Proverbs 31:11-13).

Trustworthiness

Your spouse must be able to rely upon your integrity, ability, character and truth. When you represent God's order in this manner, you generate an atmosphere of peace and comfort.

You must use your knowledge of your spouse to do him good. Never allow yourself to transmit inappropriate conversation or behavior. You must lovingly assure your spouse that he can trust you with how he feels and what he thinks. Remember! You are not in contention with him. Show him that you respect his manhood. Do not demoralize him by comparing him to other men who you might perceive "has it going on! "

He is your man! You are his helper (*even if he does not think he needs help*). Help him be the best man he can be. Communicate your desire to see him become all the man God has created him to become. You might ask, "How do I help someone that does not want help? " It is not easy; nevertheless, you can manage the spirit of your spouse. In no way does this suggest deceit or manipulation...It suggests the mastery to know your spouse and to know how to respond to him in a way that is fruitful. By doing so, *he has no need for spoil.*

When you represent the virtuosity of womanhood, you can unlock the doors of obscurity in your man's life. Your verbal and non-verbal responses to him are very important.

Look again to one of the greatest love stories ever written (Songs of Solomon). Observe how the Shulamite woman responded to the unrest of her most loved spouse.

Her management of His spirit:

Her spouse had returned from the countryside with expectations of seeing her. He arrived at the palace. He knocked! He called for Her! Her response was, "I have already gone to bed." Does this sound familiar?

When she realized that it was the one whom she much loved, she arose from her sleep. Then she went to the door only to find a gift that he had left for her. She looked around but could not see him! She then called for him but he did not answer! She did not roll over and go back to sleep! The giver was more important to her than the gift. She knew him well enough to know that this was no "small thing." She commenced to search for him. You might say, "Why go through all that?" He's overreacting! He'll get over it! Well, you see! She was in love with him. Solomon's song said she was *lovesick* (italics mine). She knew him well enough to know his response to conflict.

"My lover has gone down to his garden, to the beds of spices, to browse in the gardens and to gather lilies. I am my lover's and my lover is mine; he browses among the lilies (Solomon's Song 6:2-3 NIV)." Her management of his spirit in this situation restored the unity in their relationship. You can do the same thing.

Industriousness

One of the greatest strains on marital relationships is the mismanagement of the family's resources. This mismanagement is much larger than just finances. It does not take long to realize that financial difficulties can create barriers within your marriage. Your home is your industry or assigned duty. You have a direct responsibility helping your home realize it's full potential.

 Every wise woman buildeth her house: but the foolish plucketh it down with her hands (Proverbs 14:1 KJV).

How do you build this house? Here are a few suggestions.
- Know the needs of your house
- Develop plans for meeting those needs
- Only use material (conversation, behavior) that will reflect the quality of house you want to build
- Be prudent in how you spend the money needed for your house
- Be creative! Take the bare essentials and make something much greater

It requires much diligence to maintain a house once you have built it. It is not enough to sit back and boast about how well you built the house. A house not properly maintained will diminish in value.

Diligence

Your family depends upon your strength and honor. God has placed within you the measureless ability to "weather the storms." Perhaps the husband and the children do not respond the way they should.

Do not grow weary. The Bible says, "You will rejoice in time to come (Solomon's Song 31:25). " Are you wondering what is there to rejoice about? Well, wonder no more!

 Her children arise up, and call her blessed; her husband *also*, and he praiseth her (Proverbs 31: 28 KJV).

Your diligence will earn praise and honor from those who love you. They will place value into your dependable character and commitment.

When both male and female have fulfilled their responsibility to God's divine order, they will bring such responsibility to their marital relationship. They then can move on to experience true communion with God, as well as, one another.

Communion

Communion is the ultimate realization of belonging in your marriage. It is all encompassing. Communion involves uninhibited sharing of your thoughts; feelings and ones total being with your spouse. It is a responsive love that shares regardless to circumstances.

In Chapter 2, Created to Cleave...Not Compete, I essentially expounded upon communion when I talked about blessings, oneness, nurturing and edification. This is most important to a healthy marriage. However, I would be remiss if I did not mention the importance of physical communion.

Herein is the essence of physical communion within marital relationships:

 The husband should fulfill his marital duty to his wife, and likewise the wife to her husband. The wife's body does not belong to her alone but also to her husband. In the same way, the husband's body does not belong to him alone but also to his wife. Do not deprive each other except by mutual consent and for a time, so that you may devote yourselves to prayer. Then come together again so that Satan will not tempt you because of your lack of self-control (I Corinthians 7:3-6 NIV).

Communion is just as much spiritual as it is natural. Notice how I avoid the word sex. I encourage you to do the same. You must see physical communion for more than just an erotic urge or instinct that manifests itself in behavior.

In giving explicit instructions on Christian marriage (I Corinthians 7:3-6 NIV), the Apostle Paul emphasizes the duty of physical communion, as well as, the result to deprivation of physical communion.

God made male and female as a gift for one another; therefore, they both have a mutual moral obligation to one another. When you decided (decide if you're not already married) to marry, you relinquished authority over your body. You should make yourself available for the pleasure of your spouse.

God wonderfully made you as a powerful and influential instrument in order to make love full and complete. I must say that an instrument when improperly used can be very destructive. Avoid at all cost the temptation of using your body to manipulate or control your spouse's behavior. Perhaps I am being too diplomatic here! Let me just say, "Do not use the frequency or lack of sex as a tool in order get your spouse to do what you want them to do!" The results are disastrous. You might get what you want but there is an invisible deterioration to the foundation of your relationship.

You should not be thoughtless and abuse your right to one another. Neither should you be neglectful and ignore the needs of one another.

I mentioned earlier that marriage is a triune institute designed to have Christ as the head. When spouses abandon God's order, Satan becomes the head. He deceitfully influences decisions and behavior that will ultimately lead to separation.

Sexual love is that pinnacle expression of identification with your spouse. You become one mentally, emotionally and physically. When you willfully deprive your spouse of this oneness, Satan cunningly awaits to sow seeds of discord in your relationship. He will suggest all kinds of distortions in order for you to take your eyes off your responsibility for availing yourself to the needs of your spouse. Distortions such as:
- I do not feel like it
- It is not a good time
- I am too tired

- I need to take care of the children

Distortions! These are just a few. I am sure you may have (I mean know of...) a few. Regardless to the reason, you are depriving your spouse. Satan will cunningly present some other vice to fill that void.

The only Biblical reason for withholding yourself from your spouse is that you mutually consent to do so. This consent should be because you want to spend total consecrated time with God. You should not use this as a prolonged excuse for abstinence. Remember! Satan took advantage of Adam and Eve's separation in the garden and will do the same with you.

Physical communion is like "Icing on the Cake." Icing, however sweet, does not constitute the cake. It covers and enhances; nevertheless, it is only one ingredient.

When spouses fulfill their responsibility to God's Order through commitment and communion, communication becomes much easier. Put it all together: Oh how sweet it is!

Communication

Communication is verbal and non-verbal interaction with another.

But to do good and to communicate forget not: for with such sacrifices God is well pleased (Hebrews 13:16 KJV).

I have had many people say to me, "One of the main problems they have with their spouse is communicating." Effective communication is essential to a fulfilling marital relationship. You must seek to understand and be understood.

There are many barriers to communication. Some are more obvious than others are. Allow me to share a few.

❑ Social Backgrounds
❑ Religious Backgrounds
❑ Financial Backgrounds
❑ Life Experiences
❑ Opinions
❑ Moods and Temperaments
❑ Schedule

I am sure you can think of some more. Spouses generally experience trouble interacting because some of these barriers are influencing their ability to clearly send or receive a message.

Marriage is about overcoming these barriers in order to function freely and effectively as interdependent beings. You can overcome these barriers by being clear and concise when sending a message, as well as, practicing good listening skills.

Homemaking requires much effort. It is so easy to become pre-occupied with and distracted by the daily grind. You must deliberately plan time in which you minimize distractions in order to engage in meaningful conversation. You must learn to engage in small talk. Try discussing current events, community activities, etc. When you become effective in communicating the most mundane thing, you will find that you can effectively communicate the more serious events that occur within your marriage.

God is pleased when you can sacrifice your self-interest and agenda for the interest of your spouse. You must earn a 'Master's Degree' in interacting with your spouse. Learn to interact to the degree that God (The Master) compassionately interacts with humanity.

Such an interaction can move you into a level of intimacy that maintains the delight in your relationship. You now have the necessary means to "Plug the Leak before the Dam breaks."

~ CHAPTER 5 ~

PLUG THE LEAK... BEFORE THE DAM BREAKS!

One cannot expect to resolve differences if he or she remains the person that caused the difference...

I stated earlier that, "One of the greatest problems facing society today is the disintegration of meaningful relationships. The dilemma of our day is that we've become better at replacing our families than we have at improving and maintaining them."

As a society we suffer from the inability to resolve conflict in a meaningful way. It appears as though violence is the order of the day. We use anger as an excuse to hide behind an unwillingness to face our problems. Therefore, the endless cycle of conflict only gets worse.

Conflict is inevitable. More important than inevitability is your ability to manage it. It is very challenging to act responsibly in conflict especially when you do not feel responsible for creating it.

In order for you to improve and maintain your interdependent relationships you must be willing to reconcile your differences. By this I mean accept and resolve conflict as it occurs. This does not mean that you are going to agree on everything. Nevertheless, you can not allow conflict to break the cohesiveness and harmony within your relationship.

I once read a story that perhaps suggests the path of least resistance when it comes to conflict. One day Linus and Charlie Brown were walking along chatting with one another. Linus says, "I do not like to face problems head on. I think the best way to handle them is to avoid them. In fact, this is a distinct philosophy of mine. No problem is so big or complicated that I can not run away from it!"

If this is your philosophy for handling conflict, by now you have surely discovered that regardless to how far you run, the problem does not go away. The process for resolving conflict is vital. You should proactively establish ground rules for conflict resolution. Doing so is advantageous especially when you are angry.

Avoid engaging in character assassination while attempting to resolve conflict. Finger pointing and blaming does not get to the root cause of the problem.

 "Therefore, if you are offering your gift at the altar and there remember that your brother has something against you, leave your gift there in front of the altar. First go and be reconciled to your brother; then come and offer your gift (Matthew 5:23-24 NIV)."

Healthy conflict resolution is a necessity if you are to have a healthy and stable relationship. You must first resolve the conflict within yourself before you can reconcile the difference with another. You must then be willing to recycle the adversity that perhaps caused the conflict. Instead of attacking the other person, you must learn to attack the issue. You can stop the leak before the dam breaks by adhering to the following:

1. Define The Problem

2. Determine The Causes
3. Decide Upon Resolutions that are in the best interest of your relationship
4. Become a Prime Mover

Define the Problem

The Bible asks a very important question in Amos 3:3 NIV, "Do two walk together unless they have agreed to do so?" Does this mean that they will never encounter conflict? No! Does it mean that they will always share the same perspective? Certainly not! However, it is impossible to "walk together" unless there is a commitment to a shared purpose and direction. Reconciling differences is not all about compromising; it is about 'collaboration' or working together in a joint intellectual way. A great part of it is creating an environment wherein there is freedom to discuss feelings.

In order to reconcile differences you must be willing to define and communicate the conflict. You might be wondering; how do I communicate my feelings without things getting worse? Let me suggest the following communication technique as a helpful start. You should define the behavior and communicate how it makes you feel.

Example: Johnny/ Jean <u>when you do not actively listen to me</u> (Conflict), <u>I feel</u> <u>frustrated</u> (Effect).
Notice how I:
- Identified the behavior without bashing the person.

- I communicated how I felt. It is important to communicate feelings.

You must not deal with generalities when trying to define problems. You must be clear. You must be specific. Clear and specific problem definition can minimize the frustration associated with determining the causes.

Determine the Causes

In order to resolve interpersonal conflict individuals must determine the causes. When closely evaluated you will find that the causes are either "Ordinary" or "Distinct." Perhaps the diagram below (Fig.5-1) will enlighten you on evaluating causes to conflict.

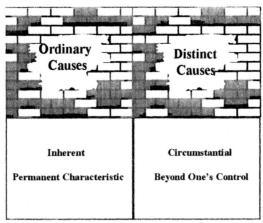

Fig. 5-1

Ordinary Causes

Ordinary problems are usually inherently woven into the fabric of one's personality or behavior. There must be a radical change in order to resolve conflict resulting from ordinary causes. Ordinary problems treated as though they are distinct will lead to oversight and neglect.

Example:

Your spouse and you hardly spend any quality time together. You bring this to the attention of your spouse. They can only offer reasons for being so busy. They might not comprehend what you are saying because the behavior is so inherent. The dilemma here is that they have treated an ordinary cause as a distinct cause. As a result, they either ignore or disregard the significance of the problem.

Distinct Causes

Distinct problems are usually beyond your control. They do not happen often and are usually governed by circumstances. It is important to understand such conflict. Distinct problems treated as though they are common will lead to frustration and overreaction.

Example:

Your spouse has had an unusually busy schedule this week. You are feeling neglected. You express as much to your spouse; however, they ask you to understand the demanding schedule. You respond by saying, "You never have time for me." Never is the key word here. You have responded to a special problem that requires special attention as if it happens all the time. As a result, you overreact and perhaps create additional problems. When conflict is mishandled or left unattended, the cracks in the wall increase. Eventually, the dam will break.

 A fool gives full vent to his anger, but a wise man keeps himself under control (Proverbs 29:11 NIV).

A fool indicates one that is deficient in judgment, sense or understanding. This is not to say that we do not get angry. However, only a person of such deficiency would allow anger to control them. Anger will impede a rational process of conflict evaluation. Careful determination and categorization of problems can lead to a meaningful and a healthy process of reconciliation.

Decide Upon Resolution

"He who cannot forgive others breaks the bridge over which he must pass himself."- George Herbert

One cannot expect to resolve differences if he or she remains the person that caused the difference. An attempt to constantly define a problem and to determine its cause could become nothing more than "nagging" when you do not approach conflict with resolution in mind.

Forgiveness must be your initial resolution. I often hear people say, "I will forgive but I will not forget." Forgiveness is essential to reconciling differences. Forgiving is an action. The American Heritage Dictionary, Second Edition, defines forgiveness as to pass over an offense and to free the offender from the consequences of it.

An unforgiving spirit is a lethal blow to conflict resolution. Let us look at the Apostles Paul's discourse on forgiveness.

If you forgive anyone, I also forgive him. And what I have forgiven -- if there was anything to forgive -- I have forgiven in the sight of Christ for your sake, in order that Satan might not outwit us. For we are not unaware of his schemes (II Corinthians 2:10-11 NIV).

Paul wrote this letter after a member of the Corinthian church had conducted himself in a reproachful way. This member had also insulted Paul's apostolic authority. Paul was deeply hurt. Through compassionate love Paul releases his offender of the offense (I also forgive him...). Paul realized that the only person that gains an advantage when you don't forgive is Satan.

What are the benefits of harboring the disappointment and pain caused by the object of your love? When you do not forgive, you grieve the Spirit of God and give place to Satan.

All of us have scars that have become a permanent part of us. We can even recall the incident that caused the scar. Nevertheless, we can choose not to recreate the pain every time we see the scar. So should our attitudes towards forgiveness be. Look at the scar if you must but release the offender. Relieve yourself of the pain!

It is not enough to simply define your problem, determine the causes. You must mutually decide on solutions that are in the best interest of your relationship. Start with deciding to forgive:

- Forgive for you partner's sake...lest he or she be overtaken by sorrow. Forgiveness is the medicine that helps to heal the broken heart.
- Forgive for Christ sake. We honor Christ when we forgive others as he has forgiven us.
- Forgive for the sake of your relationship. Do not give Satan the advantage within your relationship. Forgive with a compassionate heart and clear conscious.

After choosing the solution, you must be willing to take the necessary action.

Becoming A Prime Mover

"Gardens are not made by singing "Oh, how beautiful," *and sitting in the shade." - Ruyard Kipling*

A prime mover is something or someone regarded as the initial source of energy directed toward a goal. You must not wait for your partner to initiate the reconciliation process. Reconciliation is about you expressing your willingness to free the offender of his debt. You cannot control your partner's response. However, when you forgive, you plant seeds and cultivate the grounds which can yield peace and happiness.

Remember! Do not destroy the bridge that you too must someday cross. If you want God to forgive you, you must decide to forgive.

Reconciling differences is a natural sweetener that will aid in keeping the "Honey in the Moon."

~ CHAPTER 6 ~

KEEPING THE HONEY IN THE MOON!

Romance is a learned behavior not an inherent ability...

*W*hen I consider the state of many relationships, I can not help thinking of a premier
relationship in Ezekial 37 that had dried.
There was no "honey in the moon." The whole house
of Israel's Bones were dry...They felt that there was
no hope for their condition...They were cut off from
the grace of being one with God. They had failed to
rekindle their attraction and devotion to the
Sovereign Lord. As a result they could not respond
to nor benefit from God's everlasting love, peace and
joy. Their bones did not bolster neither did their
tendons and flesh take form until they received the
word of the Lord. The Spirit of the Lord brought life
to the body.

Can your bones live again? Is there hope for
your fragile condition? Can you realize the joy and
fulfillment you so deeply long for? Can you keep the
"honey in the moon?" For sure you can!

All that I have said until this point is the
foundation to a lasting and fulfilling interdependent
relationship...Just as the bones or skeletal structure
are the foundation to the body's composition. In
order for your body to serve you well, you must
maintain its health. Your interdependent relationship
is no different. If it is to remain healthy and fruitful
you must continue to ingest the proper foods and
indulge in consistent exercise.

An effectively maintained love relationship is
like a well-balanced triangle. Each side represents an
indispensable ingredient. Communication is the base

of the triangle. Intimacy constitutes the left side as does passion the right side (Fig. 6-1). Communication forms a stable base.

COMMUNICATION

Fig. 6-1

In Chapter 4, I talked about the essence of communication within your marriage. Now, I would like to share two other essential elements to keeping your relationship alive and fruitful. Those elements are Intimacy and Passion.

Intimacy

Intimacy does not happen automatically and is not generic. It requires constant alertness and responsiveness to your partner. Intimacy involves the creation of time and will. It is an essential expression of one's inner self. It depicts a special quality of emotional, physical and spiritual closeness between two people.

Emotional Intimacy

You can manifest emotional intimacy when you subject yourself to the feelings of your partner. You must not become callused with regard to their feelings. You must seek to understand more so than being understood. You may not actualize their feelings; however, you can empathize with them.

Therefore all things whatsoever ye would that men should do to you, do ye even so to them: for this is the law and the prophets (Matthew 7:12 KJV).

We often refer to this scripture as the "Golden Rule." What makes it so Golden?

Many think this simply suggests that one should not do wrong to anyone if he or she does not want wrong done unto them. More importantly, it suggests being proactive in goodness and mercy. It means that you must be willing to "wear the shoe on the other foot."

You can develop emotional intimacy by spending time discussing heart-felt feelings. Notice that I did not say to discuss another's thoughts but another's feelings.

The more you can identify and understand how one another feels, the more likely you are to freely share those feelings. Such freedom can constantly refurbish the trust within your relationship. Do not allow yourself to judge or validate your partners feelings. Give them the comfort of expressing themselves without fearing your response.

Physical Intimacy

So many people confuse physical intimacy with sexual activity. It is vital to learn the importance of touching...A touch that says I am yours...A touch that says, "I care."

There is great power in touching! The touching that I am referring to should not leave your partner feeling like the victim of a "Hit and Run" accident or a "Fumbled Football." Be sensitive to how and where your partner enjoys being touched. If you do not know, ask! It is important that you learn how to touch your partner in ways that are meaningful and fulfilling to them.

One of the most basic needs for humanity is the need to touch and be touched. God created us with thousands of microscopic nerve endings and sensors that enable our bodies to realize the fruition of His creation.

Touching is humanity's actualization of the joy God received when he formed man and breathed into man's nostrils the breath of life. The touch of the Master is an inner most expression of himself.

Here are a few suggestions for touching:

- Practice casual contact. Look for opportunities to touch your partner in the passing of the day. Never get too busy to share a meaningful touch.
- Practice caressing your partner gently. Do not tickle; however, pay specific attention to the

sensation of the fingertips. Use a lubricant for the more sensitive areas if needed.
- Practice rhythmic abdominal breathing. Find a position that is comfortable for both of you. Make sure you are embracing one another. With your mouth slightly open, synchronically inhale and exhale.
- Practice no hands touching. The only instructions here is that you can not use your hands. I will leave the rest to your imagination!

Practice makes permanence! When you practice ways to provide meaningful touching, it becomes a meaningful and permanent part of your relationship. The ability to provide meaningful touching can invite an uninhibited emotional response from your partner that says:

ഔ൦ൽ

Your presence is quaint--Your touch is divine.
I n case you're thinking of playing me;
Play me baby, play me...play me and take your time.
Don't stop with just one note--Hit another two or three.
You can play me all day long.
Play me baby, play me...let's make perfect harmony.[1]

ഔ൦ൽ

Touching is not just one big event. It is a million little things culminated together. You can seal emotional and physical intimacy with spiritual intimacy.

Spiritual Intimacy

Spirituality is an individual matter; however, you must commit to watching and praying for your partner.

 Again I say unto you, That if two of you shall agree on earth as touching any thing that they shall ask, it shall be done for them of my Father which is in heaven. For where two or three are gathered together in my name, there am I in the midst of them (Matthew 18:19-20 KJV).

You must always remember:
- Your enemy is Satan and His many influences
- God is not the author of confusion. In Him is no division
- Where there is unity there is strength
- When you represent that which pleases Him, He will be a very present help

You must intercede for your partner. He or she does not always have the strength or discipline needed to fight off Satan's attack.

Establish times to share with your partner in Prayer, Bible study and Worship. Establish a Spiritual closeness with your partner that says:

ᏸᏫ

When you are weak, For us I will be strong.
When you are slipping, I will help you hold on.
When you are down, I will be there to pick you up.
When you are thirsty, come drink from my cup.
When your are overwhelmed, have no fear.
 You can count on me; I am always here.[2]

ᏸᏫ

Provide your partner with spiritual closeness that is sustained by the Word of God and secured through faith.

Now that you have created time and are willing to share with your partner, ignite it with passion.

Passion

A main ingredient to passion is attitude. You must have a powerful and boundless enthusiasm for the object of your love. This enthusiasm should not be contingent upon circumstances or conditions. If you do not find ways to keep the flame of desire lit, it will altogether die. You must become creative in expressing love and desire for your beloved.

Maybe you are not as romantic as your partner is; nevertheless, this does not negate their need for romance. Remember! Romance is a learned behavior not an inherent ability. It is essential if you are to "keep the honey in the moon!"

ರಿ CONCLUSION ೮ಽ

The great tragedy of life is not that men perish, but they cease to love. -W. Somerset Maugham

7here is no one answer for the disintegration of meaningful relationships. Every situation is different. Satan is yet using deception as a tool. This tool (deception) lures us into the forbidden fruit of selfishness.

It is time for you to turn a deaf ear to him. Let him know that he will not wreck havoc in your life. *Bone Of My Bone And Flesh Of my Flesh* is not about changing your beloved. The only person you can change is you. If you do what you have always done, you will get what you have always gotten.

Many times we want to see better results in our lives; nevertheless, are not willing to become what we need to become. If what you are doing is "good," do not assume everything is "fine."

Relationships require continuous education. One can not think that love is all he or she needs. Just as you learn to love an individual you must also learn to live and function with them inter-dependently. Interdependence is not abandonment of individuality. It is the intwinement of individuality in order to experience the joy of sharing love, life and legacy.

Life is an adventure! It is important that you have the proper guidance when considering the path that you are to take. Who better to guide you than the one who created you and knows all about you?

You do not have to live beneath your God appointed privilege. Take control of your interdependent relationships by adhering to God's order for your life. Live to fulfill his divine purpose in you.

Remember! In order to love a person you must first know like and trust them. Such knowledge will constitute a friendship that can be unparalleled. Friendship is the foundation for growth in interdependent relationships.

Should your friendship grow into a companionate love affair, you must cleave to the object of your love and leave any influence that is not in the best interest of your relationship. Allow Christ's preeminence to be the perfect example for your growth. You must think and act as one. The greatest threat to your success is your selfish unwillingness to put the needs of your partner before your own.

It would be asinine to think that your relationship will never encounter conflict. How you handle conflict is most important. You must be willing to reconcile your differences in a spirit of love and meekness. Every trial you encounter is not meant to break the harmony within your relationship. Conflict can teach you how to love in a greater way if you choose to use it in that manner. Allow your love the freedom to turn away from evil and hold on to the good.

Every interdependent relationship goes through a continuous cycle of excitement, frustration and indecision. Do not accept mediocrity! Do not allow your relationship to slip into the dungeon of intimacy, you can maintain a growing and fulfilling relationship.

If you are thinking, "This all sounds good," you should try it! It is good! God intends for you to experience the love, joy and peace in sharing your life with another. May His richest blessings become yours as you grow into vessels of honor...fit and meet for the Master's use...prepared unto every good work. Make His vision for your life a reality!

Appendix

Many times people do not know where to go and get immediate resources relevant to their conditions within interdependent relationships.

Keys to the Word are biblical counsels on the subject matters written in this book. Allow the *Keys to the Word* to counsel and support you as you grow in interdependency and become all that God created you to become.

Bone Of My Bone And Flesh Of My Flesh

Notes

Chapter 2
[1] Dr. Ed Wheat, MD. *Love life for Every Married Couple.*
Zondervan Publishing House, p. 107
[2] Ricky D. Allen, *I Am Listening, Reflections Within*
[3] Stu Weber, *Four Pillars of A Man's Heart.* Multnomah Books,
p.38,39
[4] Stu Weber, *Four Pillars of A Man's Heart.* Multnomah Books,
p.41

Chapter 3
[1] Serenity Prayer
[2] Charles R. Swindoll, Improving Your Serve. Word Publishing,
p.38,39
[3] Leo F. Buscaglia, *Born for Love.* New York: Fawcett Columbine,
p.36

Chapter 4
[1] Arlene F. Saluter and Terry A. Lugaila. Marital Status and
Living Arrangements: March 1996
[2] The Quest Study Bible, New International Version

Chapter 6
[1] Ricky D. Allen, *Play Me, Reflections Within*
[2] Ricky D. Allen, *Count On Me, Reflections Within*

About The Author

*R*icky Allen is founder and pastor of the Immanuel Family Worship Center of Jacksonville, Arkansas. He is an ordained minister of the gospel who has been preaching since the age of seventeen. Ricky has served as trainer, facilitator and internal consultant in the areas of process improvement and organizational effectiveness for one of the nations largest electrical utilities. He attended the University of Arkansas at Monticello. His heart for relationships is reflected as he leads, teaches, and counsels. He is an extraordinary motivator and communicator!

To order additional copies of *Bone Of My Bone And Flesh Of My Flesh*, please complete the information below.

Ship to: (please print)

Name _____

Address _____

City, State, Zip Code _____

Day Time Phone Number _____

_____ Copies of *Bone Of My Bone And Flesh Of My Flesh*

_____ @ $10.00 each $ _____

Postage and handling @ 2.50 per book $ _____

Total amount enclosed $ _____

Make checks payable to (Immanuel Family Worship Center of Jacksonville)

Send tax deductible donation to: Immanuel Family Worship Center
Attn: Building Families Ministry
P.O. Box 5437
Jacksonville, AR 72078

To order additional copies of *Bone Of My Bone And Flesh Of My Flesh*, please complete the information below.

Ship to: (please print)

Name _____

Address _____

City, State, Zip Code _____

Day Time Phone Number _____

_____ Copies of *Bone Of My Bone And Flesh Of My Flesh*

_____ @ $10.00 each $ _____

Postage and handling @ 2.50 per book $ _____

Total amount enclosed $ _____

Make checks payable to (Immanuel Family Worship Center of Jacksonville)

Send tax deductible donation to: Immanuel Family Worship Center
Attn: Building Families Ministry
P.O. Box 5437
Jacksonville, AR 72078